*If someone were to ask me
what has been my biggest
accomplishment in life,
I would lift my head high
and speak from my heart
with a parent's pride
as I said the words
"my son."*

— Andrea Adaire Fischer

A Son Is Forever

A Blue Mountain Arts® Collection
of Writings from a Proud Parent
to a Wonderful Son

Edited by Gary Morris

Blue Mountain Press™
Boulder, Colorado

Library of Congress Control Number: 2002091705
ISBN: 0-88396-646-8

We wish to thank Susan Polis Schutz for permission to reprint the following poems that appear in this publication: "My Son," "To My Son, with Love," "To My Son, I Love You," "My Son, I Will Always Do My Best for You," and "My Son, Always Remember How Proud I Am of You and How Much I Love You." Copyright © 1983, 1988, 1989, 1991 by Stephen Schutz and Susan Polis Schutz. All rights reserved.

ACKNOWLEDGMENTS appear on page 64.

Certain trademarks are used under license.

Manufactured in China.
Second Printing: 2003

 This book is printed on recycled paper.

This book is printed on fine quality, laid embossed, 80 lb. paper. This paper has been specially produced to be acid free (neutral pH) and contains no groundwood or unbleached pulp. It conforms with all the requirements of the American National Standards Institute, Inc., so as to ensure that this book will last and be enjoyed by future generations.

Blue Mountain Arts, Inc.
P.O. Box 4549, Boulder, Colorado 80306

Contents

Son, If I Could Have Anything in the World...

I'd wish that you would
always be happy, forever healthy,
and that your life would be filled
with all the things that bring you
laughter and love.

I wish for you a life where
your dreams come true
and your goals are achieved;
I wish that I could always
wipe any tears from your face
and make everything okay again.

I hope you will always know
that I am thinking about you
and forever wanting nothing more
than your complete happiness in life.
It's your happiness that brings me
such immense joy,
because you are my son
and I love you so much.

— Shelly Gross

My Son, Always Remember How Proud I Am of You and How Much I Love You

You are growing up to be
an incredible young man
You are very unique and special
and I know that
your talents will give you
many paths to choose from
in the future
As you grow up, my son
always keep your many interests —
they will keep you
constantly occupied
Always keep your positive outlook —
it will give you the energy to
accomplish great things
Always keep your determination —
it will give you the ability
to succeed in meeting your goals

Always keep your excitement
about whatever you do —
it will help you to have fun
Always keep your sense of humor —
it will allow you to
make mistakes and learn from them
Always keep your confidence —
it will allow you to take risks
and not be afraid of failure
Always keep your sensitivity —
it will help you to understand
and do something about
injustices in the world
As you continue to grow
in your own unique, wonderful way
always remember that
I am more proud of you
than ever before and
I love you

— Susan Polis Schutz

A Very Special Poem for My Son

Son, right before my eyes, you have grown up so much on your way to becoming the special person you are today.

From a baby, to a boy, to a young man, you were full of life and filled with surprises. Trying to keep up with you has been many things: rewarding, challenging, hopeful, and fulfilling. In every one of your years, you have given me more happiness and love than most people will ever dream of.

As a family, we have walked along many paths on our way from yesterday to where we are today. Love has always been our companion, keeping us close even when we've been apart.

You have given me many gifts on that journey. But none are more precious, Son, than the smiles you give to my heart.

— Marin McKay

Someone Cares About You, and That Someone Is Me!

If you're wondering whether anyone is thinking about you now, caring about what you're doing, wishing you the best, and remembering you in prayer...

If you're feeling alienated from the world, with no one on your side, and you're questioning if there's another human being who would even be concerned about what's going on in your life...

Well, wonder no more. Someone is thinking of you and someone does care about you, and that someone is me.

If you're wishing you had someone who hopes that life is being good to you, that you're coping well with every challenge and reaching the goals you want to reach...

*If you're hoping that there is someone in
    your corner of the world that you could
    call on any time, someone with whom you
    could share your hopes and dreams and
    disappointments...*

*Well, don't waste your time wishing and
    wondering anymore. I'd be glad to be
    that someone. All you have to do is
    let me know and I'll be there.*

*If you need someone to talk to, to share
    your worries with, to wish for you
    perfect health, prosperity, and peace
    and happiness...*

*If you want someone to point out your good
    qualities because you just need lifting up,
    someone who would be on your side no
    matter what and who would go with you
    whatever distance you have to go...*

*Then look no further than my direction, and
    don't give it a second thought. Know
    someone is thinking of you and someone
    cares about you, and that someone is me.*

— *Donna Fargo*

I Remember, Son...

Your years of growing,
all our shared thoughts and feelings,
the carefree and happy times
a family shares.
I remember...
the joy, the tears, and the sorrow —
stormy emotions for changing times.
I remember...
the squeeze of your hand,
whispered "I love you's,"
the snapshots and memories
of time and years.
I remember...
all the ways
you've kept my life busy.
Every day,
I celebrate and honor
all the ways
you make my heart proud.

You, Son, are loving memories,
close and strong
    and celebrated.

                    — Linda E. Knight

What Is a Son?

A son is a warm spot in your heart and a smile on your lips.

In the beginning he is charmingly innocent, putting his complete trust in you.

He comes to you for a hand to hold and for the security only your arms can provide.

He shares his tales of adventure and knows how proud you are of his discoveries and accomplishments.

All his problems can be solved by a hug and a kiss from you, and the bond you share is so strong it is almost tangible.

Time passes, and your innocent little boy starts to test his limits. He lets go of your hand to race into the midst of life without thinking ahead or looking both ways.

His problems have grown along with him, and he has learned that you can't always make his life better or kiss his troubles away.

He spends much of his time away from you, and though you long for the closeness you once shared, he chooses independence and privacy.

Discoveries and accomplishments aren't as easy to come by now, and sometimes he wonders about his worth.

But you know the worth of that young man. He is your past and your future. He is hopes and dreams that have made it through each and every disappointment and failure.

In your heart, your son is precious and treasured. Together, you struggled through the years to find the right amount of independence for each new stage of his life, until finally, you had to learn to let him go.

Now you put your trust in him, leaving that son whom you hold so dear totally in his own care. You hope he always remembers that you have a hand for him to hold and arms to provide comfort or support.

Most of all, you hope that he believes in himself as much as you believe in him, and that he knows how much you love him.

— Barbara Cage

Twelve Tips to Help You Through Life

1. <u>Shine</u>... with your God-given talents.
2. <u>Sparkle</u>... with interest when you
   listen to others.
3. <u>Twinkle</u>... with a sense of humor,
   and you'll never take life
   too seriously.
4. <u>Sing</u>... to keep up your spirits.
5. <u>Pray</u>... and you'll know you're
   never alone.
6. <u>Unwrap</u>... your dreams and make
   them happen.
7. <u>Celebrate</u>... your every step to success.
8. <u>Decorate</u>... your own space and make
   it your peaceful retreat.
9. <u>Play</u>... with passion after you
   work hard.
10. <u>Exchange</u>... your doubts for hopes;
    your frowns for smiles.
11. <u>Make</u>... cookies, friends, happiness.
12. <u>Believe</u>... in the spirit of life
    and in your power to make the
    world a better place.

— Jacqueline Schiff

To My Son, with Love

A mother tries to provide her son
with insight into the important
   things in life
in order to make his life
as happy and fulfilling as possible

A mother tries to teach her son
to be kind and generous towards other people
to be honest and forthright at all times
to be fair, treating men and women equally
to respect and learn from older people
to know himself well
to understand his strong and weak points
to accept criticism and learn from his mistakes
to have many interests to pursue
to have many goals to follow
to work hard to reach these goals

A mother tries to teach her son
to have a strong set of beliefs
to listen to his intelligence
to laugh and enjoy life
to appreciate the beauty of nature
to express his feelings openly
   and honestly at all times
that he does not always have to be strong and stoic
that he should not be afraid to show his emotions
to realize that love is the best emotion
   that anyone can have
to value the family unit as the basis of stability

If I have provided you with an insight
into most of these things
then I have succeeded as a mother
in what I hoped to accomplish in raising you
If many of these things slipped by
while we were all so busy
I have a feeling that you know them anyway
And as your proud mother
I will always continue to love and support
everything you are and everything you do
I am always here for you, my son
I love you

— Susan Polis Schutz

You'll Always Be a Joy to Me

You'll always be love cradled in my heart
and memories to cherish through the years.
You'll always be a sunbeam, smiles for the soul,
and hugs reaching up to outstretched arms.
You'll always be the cord that binds
    and ties the years.
You'll always be dreams gently growing
    into flowers
in a garden of special secrets to share.
You'll always be footsteps racing through time
beneath the moon of yesterday.
You'll always be kisses blowing in the wind
on a playground stretched out from sky to sky.
You'll always be the gift God has given me
and years growing onward, full and deep.
You'll always be my joy, my happiness,
    my song.
You'll always be the son I love.

— Linda E. Knight

My Son, I Will Always Do My Best for You

Sometimes it is so hard
to be a parent
We never know for sure
if what we are doing or
how we are acting is right

Sometimes it might seem
like I make a decision
that is not fair
I might not be
looking at the immediate results
but I am thinking
how it will affect you
and what you will learn from it
in the future

Since I consider you
a very smart person
capable of leading your own life
I very rarely
make decisions for you
But when I do
I want you to know that
I have a great amount of
sensitivity to who you are and
the foundations of any suggestions
I give to you
are made with
an enormous love and respect
for you
my son

— Susan Polis Schutz

If I Could, Son...

If I could bring you a world full of happiness, I would. If I could take your sadness and pain and feel them for you, I would. If I could give you the strength to handle the problems that this world may have for you, I'd do that, too. There is nothing that I wouldn't do for you to bring laughter instead of tears into your life.

I can't give you happiness, but I can feel it with you. I can't take away all your hurts in this world, but I can share them with you. I can't give you strength when you need it the most, but I can try to be strong for you.

I can be there to tell you how much I love you. In times when you feel you need to reach out to someone, I can be there for you, not to change how you feel, but to go through these times with you.

When you were little, I could hold you in my arms to comfort you, but you'll never be too grown up for me to put my arms around you. You are so very special to me, and the most precious gift I could have ever received was you on the day you were born. I love you!

— Millie P. Lorenz

Son, I Want to Share These Thoughts with You

No matter where you go in this world,
here are a few things
I hope you'll remember...

Always hold honor as a high virtue.
  Despite how the world may be,
  rise above.
Always speak the truth, because others
  will hold you in high esteem as a
  man who can be trusted.
Never lose faith in your fellow human
  beings, despite times when they
  may let you down. Never forget
  to thank God for the opportunities
  you've been given.

*Believe in hard work. No one will hand
    you the future you want. The ladder
    to success is steep, but take one step
    at a time and you'll get to the top.
No matter where you go or what
    mistakes you make, remember that
    your family will always be here for
    you. That's how deep love goes.
Always believe in yourself. Your
    happiness depends on no one else
    but you. If there is something that
    you are unhappy about, you must
    change it.
Always hold love close to you. When
    you make a commitment, cherish it
    for the rest of your life.*

— *Sherrie L. Householder*

Know What It Means
to Be a Man, My Son...

A man is someone who realizes
    that strength of character
is more important than being tough.
He can be tender and kind,
    and he doesn't misuse his authority.
He is generous, and enjoys
    giving as well as receiving.
A man is understanding;
    he tries to see both sides
      of a situation.
He is responsible;
    he knows what needs to be done,
      and he does it.
He is trustworthy;
    his word is his honor.
He loves humor, and looks
    at the bright side of things.
He takes time to think
    before he reacts.
He loves life, nature, discovery,
    excitement, and so much more.
He is a little boy sometimes,
    living in an adult body
and enjoying the best of both worlds.

— Barbara Cage

...But Don't Ever Let Go of That Little Boy Inside

*Within the soul of every man
lives the little boy he once was —
a boy who looked at the world
    through eyes of wonder
and always hungered for new sights
    and far-off horizons;
who woke up each morning
    bursting with energy
and anticipation for the day ahead;
who believed in "once upon a time..."
and planned to conquer the world
    before dinner.
Don't ever let go of this little boy.
Let his spirit reawaken you
to all the potential that exists
    in your life.
Remember how it felt to believe
    you could be or do anything
        you imagined,
and bring some of that same power
    to your life today.
Honor the little boy within you...
and he will help you to become
    the great man you're meant to be.*

— Edmund O'Neill

You Deserve
Life's Best

No one is more deserving of life's rewards than you. You're a wonderful young man with a heart that is caring and compassionate. You make me very proud to be a parent. That's why nothing could make me happier than to see you receive the things your heart desires.

Every parent wants the best for their child, and I'm no exception. If I could give you the world, I would. But the reality is that nothing comes easily in life; hard work and a positive attitude are essential. And I know you're capable of both — you've already shown that.

It's easy to become discouraged at some points in your life, but the key is not to let it weigh you down. As long as you have peace about the direction your life is taking and who you are as a person, all obstacles will soon become invisible, and your dreams will become more clear.

— T. L. Nash

To My Son,
as You Grow Older

*When you were small, I
told you that someday you would
grow taller than me. And you have.*

*But you have grown in so many
more ways than just height.*

*As you have grown, you
have developed a deep sense of
caring and compassion.*

*You show a witty and
lighthearted side.*

*You're talented and productive
and never hesitate to lend a
hand to someone who may
need it.*

*You're a good friend to many
and such a wonderful son.*

*I hope that even though you
are taller than me now, you can
still look up to me, because I'm
proud of the person you've
become. I certainly look up to
you... and I imagine I always will.*

— Donna Gephart

From the Heart
of a Parent...

I thought I knew what love was all about
until the day you were born.
Suddenly, I felt an instant swell
of pride and joy within my heart.
My thoughts were overwhelmed
    with fierce protection,
future plans and hopes,
and dreams for your happiness.
I thought I knew what love was all about
until your hand reached up for mine.
You followed in my every footstep
and listened to my every word,
until I realized that my directions
    would lead your baby steps
into that greater pathway for your life.
I thought I knew what love was all about
until the day came when you asked my opinion
and sought my guidance —
considering me not only a parent,
    but also your friend.

Each moment of your life convinces me
that as time passes,
the more reasons my heart finds
to feel pride and joy in you,
and the more I love you.

— *Barbara J. Hall*

I Am Inspired
by Your Light

If I could sum up my pride and joy
at having you grace my life, I'd say:
    You help make me whole.
    You help me breathe easier.
Your contribution to this world
    extends into the universe
because a love like yours
    is certainly felt by more than
    those who know you.
You radiate a goodness
    and a passion for life
that is felt way beyond
    a certain circle.
It was ultimately your love
    that showed me how
    to love others.
You were the first person
    in the world
    to love me unconditionally.

Somehow the birth of you
was also the birth of me —
  of my courage, my convictions,
  my growth as a mother,
  my growth as a human being.
When you came into my life,
  a part of me opened up
  that I hadn't even known existed.
You gave my life purpose
  and meaning —
so much that I was then able
  to search out a true, good life...
inspired by your light.
My blessed son,
I adore you.
I respect you.
I know how very human you are...
yet to me, you walk with angels.

— Peggy Lane

You Hold the Greatest Gifts in Your Hands

I know I'm your parent, but believe me when I say that you already possess all the qualities you'll ever need in this life. You're strong willed and intelligent. You're kind and considerate. You make people feel good just by being around them.

I have complete faith in you, because I know that whatever choices you make in life will be the ones that are best for you.

So you see, you have no reason to ever be afraid of failing because in my eyes,

You're Already a Success!

— Jane Andrews

As You Go Through Life...

Remember, Son, that even when there is no path in front of you, you can always make your own. Don't be afraid to take chances or stumble, because eventually you'll get to where you want to be. It just takes time.

Even when your dreams go unfulfilled, remember that it is only temporary. You just have to be patient. Give yourself a chance to explore what life is all about and what it has to offer. Eventually, you'll see your dreams falling into place, one goal at a time.

You're dedicated, intelligent, and full of spirit, and I know you're going to have an incredible life.

I believe in you completely, and nothing you accomplish will surprise me; it will only make me proud.

— T. L. Nash

Special Wishes
Just for You, My Son

I've loved you, Son, with my whole heart and soul from the first time I counted your fingers and toes. I've loved you through your rough-and-tumble childhood and the joys and storms of your adolescence. I've loved you through tear-filled eyes when I waved good-bye as you winged your way into adulthood.

I love you today as much as I did on the day you came into the world, and I still have many of the same wishes for you...

I wish you all the things that will make you the happiest, and that you will use all the talents God gave you. I wish you the confidence to master the things that matter to you and the courage to speak your mind and heart when the majority is against you.

I wish you the discipline to reach the new goals you set for yourself and the growth of intellect and spirit that comes from surrounding yourself with good books, music, art, and people who are smart in both mind and heart.

I wish you the resilience to bounce back from suffering and begin again with your head held high. Keep on trying — give your best effort to everything you attempt.

I wish you an active life filled with respect for your body and mind. I wish you to have compassion for the suffering of others and an abundance of love to give to those who need it most.

I wish that you will always know how much I love you — from head to toe with my whole heart and soul.

— Jacqueline Schiff

You Are Perfect
Just the Way You Are

Throughout life
you will walk many paths
meet many people
and experience many things
Don't ever try to change
the person you are
to meet someone else's needs
Be yourself —
Never stop caring about the
things you value in life
and never stop striving to be your best

In front of you stands
a world of possibility
waiting to be discovered
an empty palette
longing for your touch
Be unique in your dreams
and innovative in your quest
to fulfill them

You are a beautiful shining star
Don't ever let anyone dim your light

— Deana Marino

You Have
All the Love
My Heart Can Hold

You have done so well.
You have always reached
     just a little higher and farther,
because even at a young age
you had wisdom.
As your parent, I'd like to think
that you got some of that from me,
and perhaps you did —
but there are some gifts and beautiful traits
that you alone were born with.
Ever since you were born,
there has been a light in my life
like nothing I could ever have imagined.
That light has kept me warm,
made me smile again and again,
and reminded me always
what a gift your presence has been.

It's bittersweet to watch your little boy
     become a man.
You want so much to protect him
from the dangers of the world.
You want to ward off anyone
who might cause him harm.
You want to hold his hand,
but that is not how life goes.
Today, I am confident
that the bright young man I see
will be just fine.
You have everything you need
     to face the world —
including all the love my heart
     can hold.

                        — Tim Douglas Jensen

I Want You to Be Happy

*If there is a dream in your heart...
may life bring you all the opportunities
you need to make those dreams come
true. May you also find new dreams to
inspire you and lead you on the path to
a great destiny.*

*If there is anything you need today
or any other time... may you remember
that you can always depend on me. I
promise that nothing will ever keep me
from fulfilling this commitment to you.*

*Nothing will ever be more important
to me than you and your ultimate
happiness. In every way you hope for,
may all your wishes come true.*

— Edmund O'Neill

Son, I'm Always Here for You

I know that you have everything
in your life under control.
You're doing fine, and nothing is
bothering you or standing in
your way right now.
There's no way to describe
this feeling of pride in my heart
for the way your life is going.

But I felt like reminding you once more,
the way that parents like to do,
that I'm still here to listen
when you feel like talking things over
or if you need someone to lean on for a while.
You'll always be my son,
and I'll love and care about you
your whole life through.

— Barbara J. Hall

In Admiration
of You, My Son

If someone were to ask me
what has been my biggest
     accomplishment in life,
I would lift my head high
and speak from my heart
     with a parent's pride
as I spoke the words
     "my son."
I would speak about the good fortune
     and blessing of having a son
who spreads happiness and comfort
to all who cross his path;
a son who put the concerns of others
     ahead of his own;
a son who has grown from
     an enchanting young boy
into a compassionate, courageous man;
a son who has grown up knowing
the value of respect
and who has earned the admiration
     of those who know him.

You have so many wonderful qualities
that my words to describe them
    would be endless —
much like my pride in you.
You have given so much joy
    to my life,
and I am overcome with feelings
    of tranquillity
whenever I think about who and what
    you've become.
You are my biggest and greatest
    accomplishment.
You have given my life more meaning
    and happiness
than you could ever know.
I love you.

— *Andrea Adaire Fischer*

Son, Remember This...

I'll always love you. Remember... as you read these words, that I'll hold you in a very precious place in my heart — not just today, but as long as there are stars in the sky.

Remember that — if I could — I would give you the moon and the sun in return for all the smiles and memories you've given me.

And remember that when I say "I love you," I want you to know what those words really mean. "I love you" means that you're the most wonderful son there could ever be. It means that you have made me more proud of you than you could even begin to imagine. And it means that I will never let a day go by without feeling blessed by the giving... of a gift like you.

— Laurel Atherton

You're the Best
Son in the World!

I couldn't ask for a better son. You listen. You show your appreciation. You are honorable. You have a giving heart and a loving spirit. I believe these are the best gifts we can possess to nurture our lives and help us to be of service to others.

You search your heart and try to practice the golden rule. You treat others with respect and gentleness. You seem to know instinctively that to do good things in the world, we must start with ourselves, making the grade one thought and one behavior and one action at a time. You're slow to anger, slow to judge, and quick to forgive.

You don't go along with the crowd just because it's popular, and you give others the benefit of the doubt. These are valuable qualities, and I realize I may be prejudiced, but I am proud to see these virtues in you and pleased to call you my son.

So, keep on doing what you're doing and being who you are. I'm so proud of you, Son, and I would sing your praises to anyone. I just wanted you to know how thankful I am for you. It gives me great pleasure to have you as my son.

— *Donna Fargo*

My Son

From the day you
were born
you were
so special
so smart
so sensitive
so good
It was fun
to be with you

As you grew
you became your
own person
with your own ideas
with your own way
of doing things
It was exciting
to watch you

As you grew more
you became independent
still special
still smart
still sensitive
still good
I am so proud
of the person you are
and I want you to always know
that I devotedly love you

— Susan Polis Schutz

Poems to Help My Son Be Strong Along the Path of Life

"*A*lways keep your goodness
and never lose your love.
For then, Son, you'll be
rewarded with success
in ways you never dreamed of."

"You can be head and shoulders above the crowd.
You don't have to be a giant to be strong.
Walk tall and be proud. All you have to be…
is someone people look up to."

"In the course of time, you will be reminded
that hard work gets good results and keeping
healthy is essential. Know when to work your mind
and let your body relax, and know when doing just
the opposite makes the most sense. Being able
to handle whatever life brings your way
is not a matter of coincidence."

"You've already got a good idea of what is expected of you and wished for you. One of the best things you can accomplish on life's pathway is to be a walking example of the golden rule. Don't let anyone fool you into thinking that it is worthless; it is one of the most valuable things you can do."

"You've got so many possibilities ahead! Don't be too quick to limit your choices of what to do, because you might limit your chances of unimagined joys that are waiting just for you."

"You've got a wonderful sense of humor and a good outlook on life. Let those qualities help to see you through when you're deciding where to go and you're not sure what to do."

"You've got a big heart. Keep it filled with happiness. You've got a fascinating mind. Keep finding new ways to grow. Keep yearning. Keep learning. Keep trying. Keep smiling. And keep remembering that a parent's love goes with you... everywhere you go."

— Douglas Richards

You're Everything
a Son Should Be

Throughout your life,
I have seen how each and every step
that you took
led you away from me
and toward your independence.
Yet often, you didn't even notice
that it was occurring.

The memories I have of you
still stir in my heart.
Sometimes, they cause me to
stop what I'm doing
and regret the quick passage of time.
I'm amazed that my little boy
now looks out at me from
a grown man's body.

As you move on to new adventures,
I'll be there to support you
and believe in you.
I am so proud of all that
you've accomplished;
you've become the type of man
I always hoped you would be.
(I just wish it hadn't happened so fast!)

— Barbara Cage

My Son, Never Forget How Much I Love You

When you were very, very small,
I used to dance with you
    cradled in my arms.
You were my precious angel,
and when I held you close,
love overwhelmed me.

I used to wonder what kind of life
    you would lead.
What would be your first word,
    your first job?
What kind of man would you become?
And would your life take you
    far away from me?

Then I'd hold you even closer.
I'd give you an extra kiss
and an extra squeeze,
and whisper "I love you" one more time.
I knew you were too young to remember
    my words,
but I prayed you would never forget them.

Now you are a man.
There are days when I still long
*   to cradle you in my arms*
and dance with you once again.
Although I miss my little boy,
I am so proud of the man you are
and of who you will become.
When I think of you,
love still overwhelms me.
And as we both grow older
and memories fade,
please never forget these words
that you were once too small
*   to remember:*
"I love you."

— *Kathryn Higginbottom Gorin*

To My Son, I Love You

I feel so fortunate to have you for a son
I love your bright face
when we talk seriously about the world
I love your smile
when you laugh at the inconsistencies in the world
I love your eyes
when you are showing emotion
I love your mind
when you are discovering new ideas
and creating dreams to follow
Many people tell me that
they cannot talk to their children
that they cannot wait for them to leave home
I want you to know
that I enjoy you so much and
I look forward to any time we can spend together
Not only are you my adored son
but you are also my friend
I am so proud of you
my son and
I love you

— Susan Polis Schutz

ACKNOWLEDGMENTS

The following is a partial list of authors and authors' representatives that the publisher especially wishes to thank for permission to reprint their works.

PrimaDonna Entertainment Corp. for "Someone Cares About You, and That Someone Is Me!" and "You're the Best Son in the World!" by Donna Fargo. Copyright © 2001, 2002 by PrimaDonna Entertainment Corp. All rights reserved.

T. L. Nash for "You Deserve Life's Best" and "As You Go Through Life...." Copyright © 2002 by T. L. Nash. All rights reserved.

Donna Gephart for "To My Son, as You Grow Older." Copyright © 2002 by Donna Gephart. All rights reserved.

Peggy Lane for "I Am Inspired by Your Light." Copyright © 2002 by Peggy Lane. All rights reserved.

Tim Douglas Jensen for "You Have All the Love My Heart Can Hold." Copyright © 2002 by Tim Douglas Jensen. All rights reserved.

A careful effort has been made to trace the ownership of poems used in this anthology in order to obtain permission to reprint copyrighted materials and give proper credit to the copyright owners. If any error or omission has occurred, it is completely inadvertent, and we would like to make corrections in future editions provided that written notification is made to the publisher:

BLUE MOUNTAIN ARTS, INC., P.O. Box 4549, Boulder, Colorado 80306.